DANGEROUS MAMMALS

HORSES

Madison Parker

Norwood House Press

Library of Congress Cataloging-in-Publication Data:

Names: Parker, Madison.
Title: Horses / Madison Parker.
Description: Buffalo, NY : Norwood House Press, 2025. | Series: Dangerous mammals | Includes glossary and index.
Identifiers: ISBN 9781684502745 (pbk.) | ISBN 9781684502752 (library bound) | ISBN 9781684502769 (ebook)
Subjects: LCSH: Horses--Juvenile literature.
Classification: LCC SF302.P375 2025 | DDC 636.1--dc23

Published in 2025 by
Norwood House Press
2544 Clinton Street
Buffalo, NY 14224

Designer: Ocean Books
Editor: Kim Thompson

Photo credits: Cover, pp. 1, 15 Rita_Kochmatjova/Shutterstock.com; p. 5 Erica Hollingshead; p. 6 Azahara Perez/Shutterstock.com; p. 7 Lucas Gojda/Shutterstock.com; p. 9 navatu/Shutterstock.com; p. 10 Muskoka Stock Photos/Shutterstock.com; p. 11 mveldhuizen/Shutterstock.com; p. 12 Annabell Gsoedl/Shutterstock.com; p. 13 Alexia Khruscheva/Shutterstock.com; p. 14 ilcsi/Shutterstock.com; p. 17 BearFotos/Shutterstock.com; p. 19 gorillaimages/Shutterstock.com; p. 21 Elena Yakusheva/Shutterstock.com

Printed in the United States of America

CPSIA compliance information: Batch #CW25NHP: For further information contact Norwood House Press at 1-800-237-9932.

TABLE OF CONTENTS

MEET THE HORSE

Horses are large **mammals** with **hooves**. They have **manes** on their long necks. Baby horses drink milk from their mothers.

TYPES OF HORSES

Arabian horses are sleek and strong. They have a curved neck and a high tail. These horses come from the Middle East. They can kick if they get scared.

Thoroughbreds are tall and slim with long legs. They live mainly in the United States and the United Kingdom. They run fast, so stand back when they are moving.

Shetland ponies are small and tough. They have thick fur and short legs. They come from Scotland. They bite and kick when they feel **threatened**.

Clydesdales are large and strong. They have long, hairy legs. These horses come from Scotland. They can knock people over **accidentally**.

Appaloosas have spots. These slim, fast horses live in the U.S. If they are surprised, they can kick.

Quarter horses are not very tall. They are **muscular**, with wide chests. These horses are common in the U.S. They move quickly, which can make them dangerous.

Friesians are big, black horses with long, wavy hair. They are from the Netherlands. Friesians need their space. They can be dangerous if you come too close without warning.

FAVORITE FOODS

Horses **graze** on grass for most of the day. It is soft and easy for them to eat.

In winter, horses eat hay. Hay is dried grass.

People also give their horses special horse feed. It has **grains** and vitamins. It keeps horses strong and healthy.

STAYING SAFE AROUND HORSES

When you are around horses, always move slowly. Speak softly so you do not scare them. Never stand behind a horse. You might get kicked.

Make sure horses can see you and hear you coming. Approach them from the side. This helps them know you are there.

If you want to feed a horse, ask a grown-up for help first. Hold your hand flat. This keeps your fingers from getting bitten.

GLOSSARY

accidentally (ak-si-DENT-lee): not on purpose; without meaning to

grains (graynz): small, hard seeds, especially the seeds of wheat, corn, rye, oats, rice, or millet

graze (graze): to feed on grass that is growing in a field

hooves (huvz): hard, nail-like coverings on a horse's feet; the feet of a horse

mammals (MAM-uhlz): animals that are warm-blooded, that have hair or fur, that usually give birth to live babies, and that produce milk to feed their babies

manes (maynz): long, thick growths of hair on the heads and necks of horses, lions, and some other animals

muscular (MUHS-kyuh-lur): having strong muscles; strong and powerful

threatened (THRE-tuhnd): in danger of being harmed

THINKING QUESTIONS

1. Why are horses mammals?
2. What kinds of food do horses like to eat?
3. What should you do if you are around a horse?
4. How are an Arabian horse and a quarter horse alike and different?
5. Where do horses live?

INDEX

ABOUT THE AUTHOR

Madison Parker spent her childhood in the city of Chicago, Illinois. A farm girl at heart, today she lives in Wisconsin with her husband and four children on a small farm with cows, goats, chickens, and two miniature horses named Harley and David. Her favorite dessert is vanilla frozen custard with rainbow sprinkles, even in the winter.